Sweetheart Abbey

J S Richardson

Contents

EDITED BY CHRIS TABRAHAM
ILLUSTRATED BY MICHELLE MCCLUSKIE
PHOTOGRAPHY BY HISTORIC SCOTLAND PHOTOGRAPHIC UNIT
PRODUCED BY ROY STEWART PRINT SERVICES
PRINTED IN SCOTLAND BY BUCCLEUCH PRINTERS LTD. HAWICK

FIRST PUBLISHED BY HMSO 1938
THIS REVISED EDITION FIRST PUBLISHED BY HISTORIC SCOTLAND 1995
REPRINTED 2001
CROWN COPYRIGHT © HISTORIC SCOTLAND 1995
ISBN 1 903570 26 3

Introduction

'Scho founddit into Galoway,
Off Cisteus (ordour) ane abbay:
Dulce Cor scho gert thaim call,
That is Suet Hart, that abbay all.
And now the men of Galoway
Callis that stede the New Abbay.'

[ANDREW OF WYNTOUN, PRIOR OF LOCHLEVEN, WRITING OF LADY DEVORGILLA'S FOUNDATION
OF THE CISTERCIAN ABBEY IN HIS *ORYGENALE CRONYKIL*, COMPOSED ABOUT 1420]

The abbey of Sweetheart was founded in 1273 by Lady Devorgilla of Galloway in memory of her late husband, John Balliol. At her own death in 1289 her body was laid to rest before the high altar and her husband's embalmed heart, her 'sweet, silent companion', placed beside her. The monks chose the beautiful name of Sweetheart, or *Dulce Cor*, for their abbey in her memory.

Sweetheart Abbey's conception as a shrine to human and divine love is deeply appealing. So too are the ruins of this once proud monastery in its peerless setting between Criffel's grey bulk and the silver waters of the Nith. Established as a daughter house of the Cistercian abbey of Dundrennan, near Kirkcudbright, Sweetheart was a place devoted to the worship of God. It was also a centre for sheep farming. This tranquil idyll was rudely broken during the wars with England in the early fourteenth century; Edward I of England, 'Hammer of the Scots', stayed there in August 1300 on his return from invading Galloway. Later in that century the monastery came under the patronage of Archibald 'the Grim', third Earl of Douglas, the builder of the forbidding Threave Castle, near Castle Douglas.

The sixteenth century witnessed the Reformation and the demise of Sweetheart. It proved a long, lingering death on account of the stubborn refusal of its last abbot, Gilbert Broun of Carsluith, to embrace the reformed religion. He defiantly resisted all attempts to remove him until 1608 when he was forced to retire to France. In 1779 some local gentlemen acquired the abbey church, by then roofless, to prevent it being used as a stone quarry as the cloister buildings had been. Their successors secured the fabric until 1928 when the abbey was entrusted into State care.

Sweetheart Abbey's majestic interior, looking eastward from the west door down the nave to the central bell tower and into the presbytery. At the far end is the great east window.

The Story of Sweetheart Abbey

DEVORGILLA, LADY OF GALLOWAY

O n 10 April 1273, Lady Devorgilla, a lady of the blood royal of Scotland, signed a charter establishing a new Cistercian abbey on a site close to where the River Nith flows into the Solway Firth and overshadowed by a great granite mountain, Criffel. Her beloved husband, John Balliol, had died four years earlier and the abbey was intended as a lasting memorial to him.

Throughout their married life, Devorgilla and Balliol, who resided at Buittle Castle, near Dalbeattie, were devoted to each other. On Balliol's death in 1269, the grieving widow had his heart embalmed and placed in a casket of ivory bound with enamelled silver. She kept this, her 'sweet, silent companion', with her until she too died in 1289 in her eighty-first year. The casket was buried with her in the sanctuary of the monastery church she had founded. It was fitting tribute to her undying love that the monks there chose the beautiful name of Sweetheart, or *Dulce Cor*, for the abbey.

At the time of Devorgilla's death, Hugh de Burgh, Prior of Lanercost in Cumberland, composed an elegy which was inscribed on the monument that marked the place of her tomb, in front of the high altar in the abbey church:

'*In Devorgilla a living fount of wisdom dies and a contemplative Mary as well as a virtuous Martha. Grant, O King most high, the attainment of rest to Devorgilla, whom, with the heart of her husband, likewise, this stone covers.*'

The effigy of Devorgilla, with the embalmed heart of her beloved husband, John Balliol, clasped to her bosom.

Sweetheart was not Lady Devorgilla's only act of patronage. In Scotland, she founded two other religious houses – friaries in Wigtown and Dundee – and two chaplaincies in Glasgow Cathedral. The attractive stone bridge over the Nith in Dumfries is also hers. Undoubtedly, her most enduring act of patronage was her confirmation and endowment of Balliol College, Oxford, in 1282, which had been established by her late husband as an act of penance. Andrew of Wyntoun, chronicling her achievements about 1420, tells us that:

'A better lady than scho was nane,
In at the Ille of Mare Brettane,
Scho was richt plesande of bewte;
Here was gret takynnys [tokens] *of bownte.'*

Devorgilla's bridge over the River Nith in Dumfries.

THE CISTERCIAN ORDER

The monks who colonised Sweetheart belonged to the Cistercian order. Their first monastery was established in 1098 at Citeaux in France (whence the name) by monks who wished to return to the more exact observance of the Rule of St Benedict as set out in Italy in the early 400s. It was a life 'shut away' from the outside world and dedicated to prayer, hard work and an uncompromising insistence on poverty, chastity and obedience. Aelred, Abbot of Rievaulx in Yorkshire, wrote:

The seal of an abbot of Sweetheart.

'Our food is scanty, our garments rough; our drink is from the stream and our sleep often upon our book. Under our tired limbs there is but a hard mat; when sleep is sweetest, we must rise at bell's bidding...Self-will has no place; there is no moment for idleness or dissipation...Everywhere peace, everywhere serenity, and a marvellous freedom from the tumult of the world.'

The Cistercians, or the 'white monks' as they were more generally known from the colour of their undyed woollen habit, first arrived in Scotland at Melrose, in Tweeddale, in 1136. They came from Aelred's Rievaulx. Six years later, a further group of Rievaulx monks arrived in Galloway and established a house at Dundrennan, near Kirkcudbright. Sweetheart, the last of the 12 Cistercian monasteries set up in Scotland, was founded by monks from Dundrennan, which is situated 18 miles (28 km) as the crow flies to the south-west.

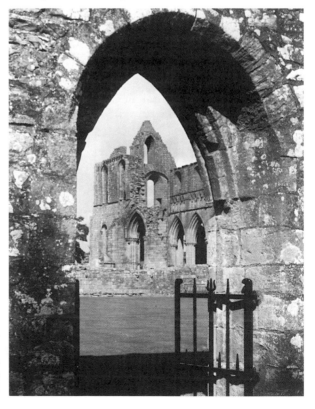

The enchanting ruin of Dundrennan Abbey, near Kirkcudbright, from where Sweetheart was founded.

THE LIFE OF THE COMMUNITY

Large monasteries, like Sweetheart, were supreme examples of order in the medieval world. This concern with order and permanence, which can be seen today in the buildings, was expressed in the life of the monks and in the organisation of the community.

The monastic life at Sweetheart, in common with Cistercian houses everywhere, was dominated by a formal pattern of worship. Normally, in summer, the first prayers were said at 1.30 in the morning, followed by a sung service, *Nocturns*. At 3.30 *Matins* was sung, then *Prime* at 6.00 at which the first mass of the day was said. After this the brethren met in the chapter house, to read a chapter from St Benedict's Rule, to confess misdemeanours, and to discuss the day's work. After a short period of work, *Terce* and sung mass followed at 8.00. There were two hours of reading from 9.30, then the service of *Sext* at 11.30 followed by the main meal at midday. After a further period of rest and prayer, the brethren again gathered in the church at 14.30 for *None*, after which they worked until supper at 17.30. *Vespers* began at 18.00. There was a light supper at 19.30, then the short service of *Compline* before the monks retired to the dormitory at 20.15.

Outside the church, the Cistercians were famed for their farming skills. 'Give the Cistercians a wilderness or forest, and in a few years you will find a dignified abbey in the midst of plenty', wrote Bishop Gerald of Wales in 1188. They specialised in agriculture and in horse and cattle breeding. They also held great interest in the wool trade. They controlled certain fisheries, and they were involved in the manufacture of salt from sea-water. Cistercian monasteries were set up on fertile land ideal for such activities, and to help them with all these activities, they had lay brothers, who were the working members of the community and took the place of servants and workmen.

Cistercian monks splitting wood, from a twelfth-century painting, a reminder that the monks themselves engaged in physical labour.

WAR WITH ENGLAND

Lady Devorgilla and John Balliol had a son, also John. In 1292, he became King of Scots, but his was to be a short, tragic reign. In July 1296 he was stripped of his regalia by the English king and the costly fur was taken from his surcoat, or tabard. The downfall of 'Toom Tabard' ('empty coat') heralded the bloody and prolonged wars with England that bedevilled the country for over 50 years. Inevitably, Sweetheart Abbey, a major land-holder in Galloway with its intimate associations with the Balliols, was drawn into the turmoil.

In 1296, John, the first abbot, paid

An image of King John Balliol with broken crown, sword and sceptre and torn tabard, symbolising the ignominious end to his reign in 1296.

homage to Edward I of England at Berwick-Upon-Tweed. The allegiance brought the abbey, briefly, into the attempts made by Edward to gain control of Scotland. In June 1300, Edward and his son invaded Galloway, taking Caerlaverock Castle on the way, and going as far as Kirkcudbright. On his return, Edward stayed at Sweetheart, and it may well have been there that he received a statement from Pope Boniface VIII demanding that the English withdraw from Scotland and asserting that Scotland belonged to the Holy See.

The army was withdrawn to Carlisle, but in the following year a larger force, led by the Prince of Wales, again invaded Galloway. Tradition has it that when the Prince proposed to visit the shrine of St Ninian at Whithorn, the Scots removed the saint's image to Sweetheart. That same night, however, being anxious to receive the offerings of the Prince, St Ninian supposedly caused the image to be miraculously restored to its shrine some 100 miles (160 km) away!

ARCHIBALD 'THE GRIM'

The arched doorway in the west cloister range with the Douglas arms (a heart and three mullets, or stars) emblazoned above.

In 1352, David II, Robert the Bruce's son and successor, returned to Scotland from a lengthy captivity in England and began the task of returning the country to prosperity. The wars with England had impoverished Sweetheart and reduced its buildings to a state of disrepair; they had also resulted in the forfeiture of the Balliols. A new patron had to be found for the abbey and King David turned to his close friend, Archibald Douglas, whom he had created Lord of Galloway in 1369. Archibald, who resided in the forbidding island fastness of Threave Castle, was more popularly known as 'Black Archibald' or 'the Grim' and had earned his by-name fighting against the English.

In a writ of 1381 Archibald is described as founder or reformer of Sweetheart, indicating that his benefactions were substantial. In 1385 he made a further grant to the abbey for prayers to be offered up for his soul and those of his parents, his wife, Joanna, and his two sons. Archibald was also patron of Lincluden Collegiate Church, near Dumfries, but after his death at Threave on Christmas Eve 1400 he was buried in neither place but in the collegiate church at Bothwell, in Lanarkshire, close to another of his formidable castles.

THE REFORMATION

During the turbulent times following the death of James IV at Flodden in September 1513, the monks of Sweetheart placed themselves and their tenants under the protection of the local magnate, Lord Maxwell. By the time of James V's death in 1542, shortly after his defeat at the hands of the English at Solway Moss, there was general concern about the 'dishonesty and misrule of kirkmen', and it is clear that the Scottish Church had become lax and ill-disciplined. As the cloud of the Reformation approached, the monks of Sweetheart, anxious to protect themselves and their property, increasingly looked to Lord Maxwell, a devout Catholic, for help. He proved an invaluable friend. When at the Reformation in 1560 the Lords of the Congregation ordered him to destroy the buildings, he refused, declaring that he was attached to the place 'quhair he was maist part brocht up in his youth'.

ABBOT GILBERT BROUN AND THE FINAL YEARS

The last abbot of Sweetheart was Gilbert Broun, of the ancient family of Brouns of Carsluith, near Creetown. Abbot Gilbert, who stolidly refused to embrace the reformed religion, was able to continue to dwell at Sweetheart only through the good offices of the Maxwells. But by the Annexation Act of 1587, Sweetheart was vested in the Crown and the obstinate cleric was forced to flee to France. He was not to be so easily removed. Two years later he returned to his old haunt and took up the fight once again. Eventually, in 1603, he was arrested and imprisoned in Blackness Castle, on the Firth of Forth, before being released into exile again.

By 1608, Abbot Gilbert was back at Sweetheart in open defiance of his King, James VI. An attempt to arrest him by the Dumfries guard failed when they were beaten off by 'a convocation of a great number of rude and ignorant people, armed with stones, muskets and hagbuts in a tumultuous and unseamlie manner'. He was eventually arrested by the King's guard but the Privy Council, taking pity on the frail abbot, permitted him to remain in his lodgings in Sweetheart. But the abbot was determined to keep the Catholic faith alive in the ancient monastery. In 1608, his chamber was broken into on the orders of the Archbishop of Glasgow and 'a great number of Popish books, copes, chalices, pictures, images and such other Popish trash' was discovered. All except the books were publicly burned on a market day in the High Street in Dumfries. Abbot Gilbert returned to France once again where he died in 1612.

Sweetheart Abbey from the south-east in the late eighteenth century. On the left is the parish church built against the south wall of the nave in 1731. (Courtesy of the Royal Commission on the Ancient and Historical Monuments of Scotland.)

THE DESTRUCTION OF THE BUILDINGS

The old name of the parish was Kinderloch and the parish church stood on an island in the loch of that name, situated in the hills a mile (1½ km) to the south of the abbey. By the seventeenth century church services were being held in the abbey in a building on the south side of the cloister, probably the monks' refectory. About this time the parish was renamed New Abbey after the name locally given to Sweetheart to distinguish it from the 'old' abbey at Dundrennan. In 1731 a new church was built against the south wall of the nave. This was demolished in 1877, by which date all but the magnificent church had been removed to provide stone for the villagers and the farming folk round about. The church had been saved in 1779 by local subscribers 'desirous of preserving the remainder of that building as an ornament to that part of the country'. In 1928 their successors entrusted the beautiful ruin of Sweetheart into State care.

A party of gentlemen in the crossing under the tower, photographed about 1860. In the background is the north transept. (Courtesy of the Royal Commssion on the Ancient and Historical Monuments of Scotland.)

A Short Tour of

1. CLOISTER
AN ENCLOSED RECTANGULAR COURT
SURROUNDED BY THE CHURCH AND DOMESTIC
BUILDINGS. AROUND THE CLOISTER WAS A
COVERED ALLEY CONNECTING THE BUILDINGS
AND SERVING ALSO AS A WORK PLACE.

2. WEST RANGE
NOW LARGELY GONE BUT ONCE HOUSING STORE
ROOMS AND ACCOMMODATION FOR THE LAY
BROTHERS. THE ARCHED DOORWAY HAS SHIELDS
ABOVE IT BEARING THE DOUGLAS ARMS.

3. SOUTH RANGE
NOW LARGELY GONE BUT ONCE HOUSING THE
KITCHEN AND REFECTORY.

4. WARMING ROOM
THE ONLY ROOM WITH A FIREPLACE DESIGNED
FOR COMFORT RATHER THAN FOR COOKING AND
WHERE THE MONKS WERE PERMITTED TO
GATHER FOR A SHORT TIME EACH DAY.

5. PARLOUR
THE ONLY ROOM WHERE THE MONKS WERE
PERMITTED TO SPEAK INFORMALLY WITH EACH
OTHER. THE SMALL ROOM OFF THE PARLOUR MAY
HAVE BEEN THE TREASURY WHERE VALUABLES
WERE STORED.

6. CHAPTER HOUSE
THE MEETING ROOM WHERE THE MONKS
GATHERED EACH MORNING TO CONFESS THEIR
SINS AND DISCUSS BUSINESS. THE SURVIVING EAST
WINDOW WAS PROBABLY ORIGINALLY IN THE
REFECTORY BUT RE-ERECTED HERE IN 1877.

7. LIBRARY AND SACRISTY
A ROOM USED FOR STORING BOOKS AND ITEMS
USED IN CHURCH SERVICES.

Sweetheart Abbey

8. SOUTH TRANSEPT
ONE OF TWO CROSS-ARMS OF THE CHURCH ONCE HOUSING SIDE CHAPELS ON THE EAST. IN THE SOUTH WALL IS A BOOK CUPBOARD. THE OPENING UP AND TO THE RIGHT OF THE DOOR LEADING TO THE LIBRARY [7] WAS REACHED BY A WOODEN STAIR AND LED TO THE MONKS' DORMITORY ON THE FIRST FLOOR OF THE EAST RANGE. THE RESTORED TOMB OF DEVORGILLA IS DISPLAYED HERE; HER DAMAGED EFFIGY LIES HOLDING HER HUSBAND'S EMBALMED HEART.

9. CHOIR
THE HOLIEST PART OF THE CHURCH, RESERVED FOR THE MONKS AND ONCE CONTAINING THEIR CHOIR STALLS. THE HIGH ALTAR STOOD IN THE PRESBYTERY AT THE EAST END. IN THE SOUTH WALL IS A RECESS (*PISCINA*) FOR RINSING THE COMMUNION VESSELS, AND THREE ARCHED SEATS FOR THE OFFICIATING PRIESTS. A MODERN STONE MARKS THE APPROXIMATE POSITION WHERE IN 1289 DEVORGILLA WAS BURIED WITH HER HUSBAND'S HEART.

10. NORTH TRANSEPT
ONE OF TWO CROSS-ARMS OF THE CHURCH ONCE HOUSING SIDE CHAPELS ON THE EAST. A SPIRAL STAIR IN THE NORTH-WEST CORNER GAVE ACCESS TO THE UPPER PARTS OF THE CHURCH AND TO THE BELL TOWER OVER THE CENTRAL CROSSING.

11. THE NAVE
FOR THE USE OF LAY BROTHERS ATTENDING SERVICES, AND ONCE DIVIDED FROM THE MONKS' CHOIR [9] BY A SCREEN. THE HEIGHT OF THE WOODEN ROOF CAN BE SEEN BY THE LINE, OR RAGGLE, MARKING WHERE IT JOINED THE CROSSING TOWER.

Artist's bird's-eye view of the abbey from the south-west.

The Architecture of Sweetheart Abbey

THE SITE

The site chosen for Sweetheart was perfect for the Cistercian way of life, quiet and secluded. Sheltered on the west by rising ground, its fertile land could be drained into a slow winding burn or pow, called New Abbey Pow, while water from two swifter running burns and from a neighbouring loch could be diverted to provide drinking water, water for fishponds and power for the cornmills. Where the deep channel of the Abbey Pow entered the wide tidal estuary of the Nith, a little more than a mile (1¹/2 km) from the abbey, was a safe and natural harbour for ships bringing in building materials and other provisions and carrying away the produce of the monastic granges.

THE PRECINCT

The abbey complex was confined within a precinct 30 acres (12 ha) in area. Its southern boundary was a great water-filled ditch, whilst the other three sides were defined by an impressive **precinct wall**, a considerable portion of which still remains. It stands over 9 ft (3 m) high in places and is built of massive granite boulders. There were two main gateways into the precinct, one in the centre of the west side and the other in the southern part of the east side. Part of the west gate is still visible near the centre of the village.

Within the precinct, the church and cloister were placed conveniently close to the west gatehouse. They were approached through an outer court around which were grouped the stores and offices, such as the guest-house, granary, brewhouse and bake-house. Near the gate-

A well-preserved stretch of precinct wall, showing the construction from massive granite boulders squared off to a face.

house was the almonry where poor visitors seeking charity were lodged and given alms. To the east of the cloister, in a secluded position near the monks' cemetery, was the infirmary, to which the elderly and infirm brethren retired and to which all in the community went periodically to be bled by leeches. The abbot's house may also have been in this area, but all traces above ground of these buildings have long gone.

Of this once-thriving monastic institution only the splendid ruins of the abbey church survive substantially complete. The lower walls of the east range and the outline of the cloister are all that remain of the monastery buildings.

An aerial view of Sweetheart Abbey from the south, with the precinct wall forming an L to the north, and continuing towards the bottom left-hand corner of this view. Sweetheart possesses the most complete precinct walls surviving round a Scottish medieval monastery.
(Courtesy of the Royal Commission on the Ancient and Historical Monuments of Scotland.)

CONSTRUCTING THE ABBEY

Although no description of the building of the monastery survives, we can put together a fairly clear picture of how it was constructed. First the land was cleared of granite boulders, some of considerable size. These were used to build the precinct wall, the domestic buildings and the cores of the church walls. The red sandstone for the church and for the window and door surrounds in the cloister buildings was brought from quarries on the eastern shore of the Nith. The massive oak timbers for the roofs and fir trees for scaffolding may have been imported by sea. Lead for roof coverings, glass for windows, and doubtless many other furnishings for the church may have been brought from England and the Continent.

As there were no architects as such in medieval times, the abbey would have been designed by a master-mason appointed by the abbot and working to general instructions from one of the monks. He was assisted by the monks, lay brothers and some skilled masons working under him. The builders lived in temporary wooden huts, as did the monks themselves until their new home was ready. Building work was concentrated initially on the east end of the church so that the important round of services could begin as soon as possible.

The architecture of the church seems to have been directly influenced by the style of Gothic which developed in France in the 1230s and was taken up in England about 20 years later.

Looking across the cloister to the abbey church. The change in the design of the windows along the top of the nave (left of the central tower) may mark the position of the internal screen, the pulpitum, *dividing the monks' and lay brothers' choirs. The crow-stepped top of the central tower was added late in the life of the abbey.*

While adhering to the austere views of the Cistercians, the church is still a fine piece of architecture with careful attention paid to details such as the stone tracery in the windows, especially in the presbytery at the east end of the choir. The master-mason was quite ingenious in his approach to problems he faced. In the south transept he had to take the roof of the monks' dormitory into account when designing the windows, and solved this neatly by using a wheel window with a segment cut out where the roof line joins the south wall. Cistercian austerity can still be seen though in the planning of the building; there is no triforium gallery between the nave arches and the windows above, and the tower over the crossing is kept deliberately low (the decorative battlements and the gables above are later additions) in deference to a ban in 1157 on bell towers.

THE ABBEY CHURCH

The abbey church at Sweetheart, in common with all Cistercian churches, was dedicated to St Mary the Virgin. It was planned in the shape of a cross and divided up into different areas. A timber screen, called a *pulpitum*, to the west of the crossing divided the lay brothers' choir at the west end, the nave, from the monks' choir to the east. There is a change in the design of the outer upper windows between the second and third bays of the nave which may mark the position of this screen. Often the construction work on abbey churches was halted following completion of the monks' choir so that work could begin on the chapter house. The completion of the church would then follow after a period of time and in a slightly different style.

The beautiful ruin of Sweetheart Abbey from the south-east. The presbytery is on the right.

The **west front** of the church, housing the main processional doorway, was dominated by a spacious window. This was originally a single glazed window with mullions (stone uprights) terminating in tracery. When disaster befell the window, presumably during the lightning that struck the abbey shortly before 1381, the window opening was reconstructed with a trefoil window at the top and a band of masonry inserted to give greater stability to the gable. On the outside of the west front, directly above the doorway, can be seen the projecting stone corbels which supported the lean-to roof of the porch, or narthex, which protected the doorway (see the reconstruction on page 23).

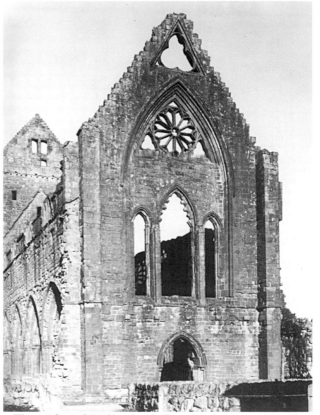

The west front of the abbey church. The corbels that once supported the roof of the narthex (processional porch) are visible above the door.

To either side of the central crossing were the **transepts** which housed additional altars in their eastern chapels. Over and above the eight set services, or offices, the monks were obliged to attend, each individual had to pray privately for the souls of those who had patronised the order. These additional altars, dedicated to other saints, were the focus of this private contemplation.

In the **north transept**, the chapel on the left has an aumbry, or wall-cupboard, in its north wall where the reserved host (the bread and wine) was held. The right-hand chapel has the remains of a *piscina*, or basin, in its south wall where the altar vessels were rinsed after the celebration of the mass. In the **south transept**, both the *piscina* and the aumbry are in the south wall. The south transept also contained the night-stair which gave access to the church from the dormitory for the monks attending the night-offices.

wall passage

door to
dormitory

wall
cupboard

door to
sacristy

position of
night stair

The south transept.

The south transept is now home to **Lady Devorgilla's monument** (see the photograph on page 4). Devorgilla had been laid to rest before the high altar in the presbytery but by the sixteenth century her original monument seems to have been destroyed. A new one was made in the form of a table on which rested the effigy of the foundress, dressed in gown and mantle and cradling a representation of her husband's heart on her breast. Fragments of this later monument were recovered during clearance work in the late 1920s and reassembled in 1932 in the south transept. The sides of the monument are ornamented with square traceried panels containing shields or badges. The remains of the inscription on the capstone reads:

[R]VILLA FUDATRIX HUI MONA [carving] STII QUE OBIIT S M CCLXXXIIII

Devorgilla fundatrix huius monasterii quae obiit 1284

(*Devorgilla, foundress of this monastery, who died 1284*)

The year of Devorgilla's death is inaccurately given. Also in the south transept chapel is the decorated coffin-lid of John, the first abbot.

The most sacred part of the church was the **presbytery** at the east end of the monks' choir where the high altar was situated. The east wall behind the high altar contained a splendid traceried window. It was here in the presbytery that the officiating priest stood to conduct the service, and sat in the *sedilia*, or arched seat, in the south wall flanked by his assistants at the mass. In the same wall, a little to the east, is the *piscina*, or basin, where the altar vessels were rinsed.

One of the ceiling bosses in the vaulting of the south transept chapels. The shield bears two crosses in saltire together with a heart and three stars (the Douglas arms). The inscription is now illegible.

wall passage

Devorgilla's
grave-marker

piscina

sedilia

The presbytery.

The windows in the north wall of the presbytery, with their fine bar tracery. Bar tracery originated in France about 1210 and Sweetheart has the finest surviving windows of this new form in Scotland.

THE CLOISTER BUILDINGS

The cloister was the monks' domestic home just as the church was their spiritual one. It lay on the south side of the church so that the high roof of the church did not block out the sunlight. The cloister had at its centre a rectangular open **garden** surrounded by the church on the north and the various buildings along the other three sides. These buildings were linked to each other and to the church by **covered walks**, or alleys. The present gravelled areas mark out these roofed alleys and buildings. The north cloister walk was also used by the monks during their periods of private study. During the day the main entrance to the church was at the north end of the east walk. This is marked out as an important door by its elaborate surround, now sadly eroded. During the night the monks came straight from their dormitory to services via the doorway in the south transept.

On the **west side** of the cloister stood the lay brothers' accommodation and the store rooms. Along the **south side** were the kitchen, the refectory where the monks ate together and in silence, and other rooms including probably the novices' room. None of these buildings now survives above foundation height, only a much rebuilt arched doorway in the west range with a draw-bar slot in its side and two armorial shields of the Douglases overhead.

The **east side** of the cloister is marginally more complete. Passing southward away from the church were the **library** and **sacristy**, the **chapter house**, the **parlour** with a small room off it which may have served as the treasury, and the **warming room**. The chapter house, the main meeting room, is the most complete. It was originally vaulted and had stone benches around the side walls where the monks sat. The abbot, or his deputy, would have sat in the centre of the east wall. The large window now in that wall began life in a building in the south range, probably the refectory, was rebuilt in the east wall of the parish church that was built on the north side of the cloister in 1731, and was only re-erected in its present position in 1877 when the parish church was demolished.

Sweetheart Abbey as it might have looked in 1350.

New Abbey Corn Mill, at the far end of the village from the abbey, is known locally as 'Monksmill'. Although the present building dates only from the late eighteenth century, it probably replaced an earlier grain mill operated by and for the monks. The mill is in working order and demonstrated regularly to visitors in the summer months.

Further Reading

D MacGibbon and T Ross *The Ecclesiastical Architecture of Scotland*, vol 2 (1896), 334-44

Wentworth Huyshe *Devorgilla, Lady of Galloway* (1913)

ON ABBEYS GENERALLY

J Bilson 'The architecture of the Cistercians', *Archaeological Journal*, 56 (1909), 185-290

I B Cowan and D E Easson *Medieval Religious Houses in Scotland* (1976)

P Fergusson *The Architecture of Solitude* (1984)

R Fawcett *Scottish Medieval Churches* (1985)

S Cruden *Scottish Medieval Churches* (1986)

R Fawcett *Scottish Abbeys and Priories* (1994)